A Color Scavenger Hunt

by Jenna Lee Gleisner

The Child's World®
childsworld.com

Published by The Child's World®
1980 Lookout Drive • Mankato, MN 56003-1705
800-599-READ • www.childsworld.com

Photographs ©: Shutterstock Images, cover (top left), cover (top middle),
cover (top right), cover (bottom left), 3 (top left), 3 (top middle), 3 (top right),
3 (bottom left), 4, 5 (top left), 5 (top right), 5 (bottom left), 5 (bottom right), 8,
10, 11, 12, 13 (top left), 13 (bottom left), 13 (bottom right), 14, 15 (top right),
16, 17 (top left), 17 (bottom left); Jenny Sturm/Shutterstock Images, cover
(eggs), 3 (eggs); Audrius Merfeldas/Shutterstock Images, cover (bottom right),
3 (bottom right), 13 (top right); Peter Hermes Furian/Shutterstock Images,
6; Dariusz Kantorski/Shutterstock Images, 7; Kiril Stanchev/Shutterstock
Images, 9; Sinan Kocaslan/iStockphoto, 15 (top left); iStockphoto, 15
(bottom left), 15 (bottom right), 19 (top right); Pino Magliani/Shutterstock
Images, 17 (top right); Mr. Nakorn/Shutterstock Images, 17 (bottom right);
Yuganov Konstantin/Shutterstock Images, 18; Hong Vo/Shutterstock Images,
19 (top left); Rose-Marie Henriksson/Shutterstock Images, 19 (bottom left);
Sergey Chayko/Shutterstock Images, 19 (bottom right); Wave Break media/
Shutterstock Images, 20; Racheal Grazias/Shutterstock Images, 21

Design Elements ©: Jenny Sturm/Shutterstock Images; Audrius Merfeldas/
Shutterstock Images; Shutterstock Images

ISBN 9781503823617
LCCN 2017944881

Printed in the United States of America
PA02361

About the Author

Jenna Lee Gleisner is an author and
editor who lives in Minnesota. She
has written more than 80 books for
children. When not writing or editing,
she enjoys spending time with her
family and her dog, Norrie.

We see colors every day. To see colors, we need light. We cannot see colors in the dark. Turn the page to find the different colors in this book!

Light shines on objects. Some colors bounce off an object. Others are **absorbed**. Our eyes only see the colors that bounce off or **reflect**.

4

Which objects reflect the color red?

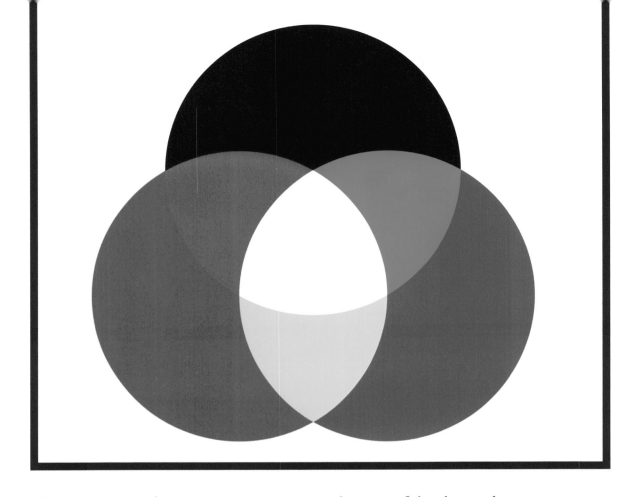

There are three **primary colors** of light. These are red, green, and blue. When these colors of light mix, they make other colors. Red and green make yellow. All of the colors of light together make white.

Which primary colors of light
do you see in this rainbow?

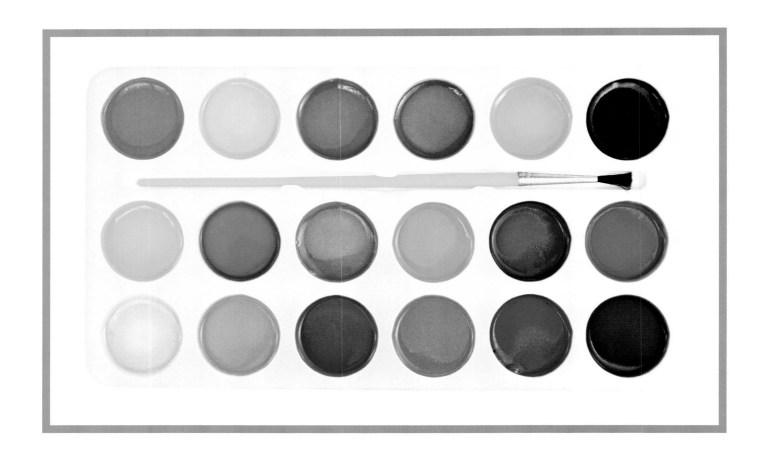

Pigment is a substance that adds color. Paint is a pigment. There are three primary colors of pigment. These are red, yellow, and blue.

Which primary colors of pigment are in this painting?

We mix primary colors to make secondary colors. These are orange, green, and violet. Red and yellow mix to make orange. Red and blue mix to make violet.

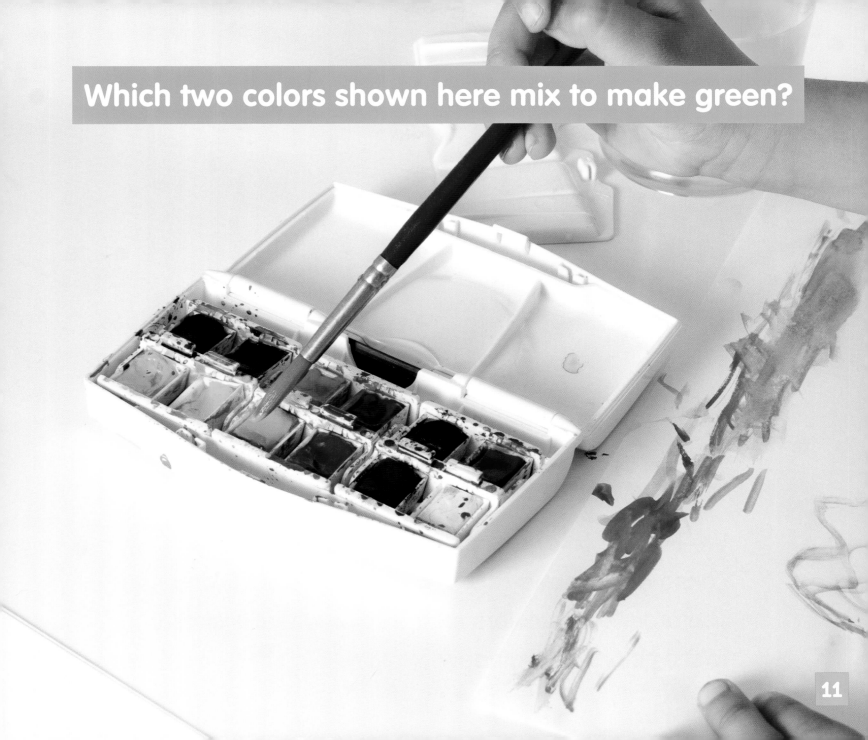

Which two colors shown here mix to make green?

11

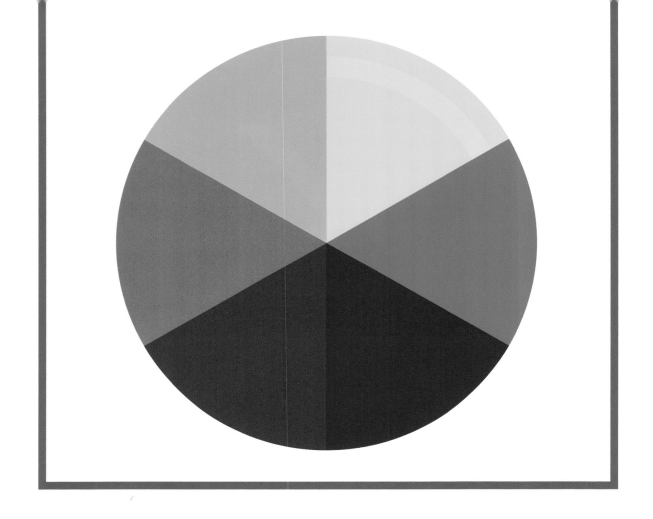

We use the **color wheel** to organize colors. The color wheel shows how colors relate to each other. The order of the colors on the color wheel is similar to the colors in a rainbow.

Which of these objects match the color wheel?

Complementary colors are opposite each other on the color wheel. These opposite colors go well together. For example, red and green are complementary colors.

Which of these team uniforms has complementary colors?

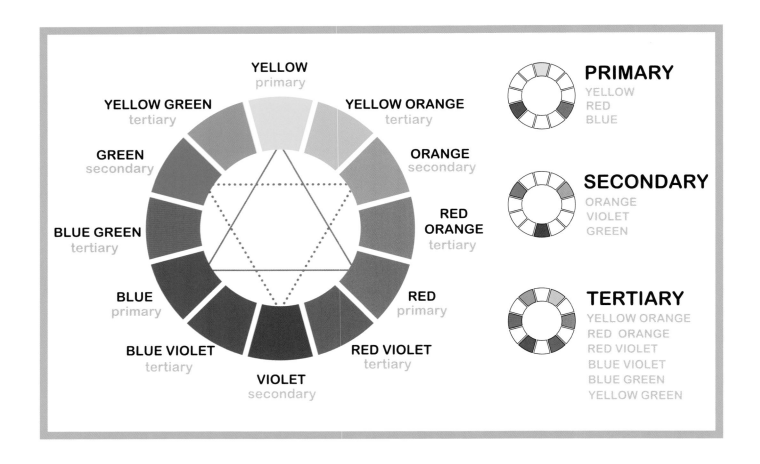

Tertiary colors are made by mixing an equal amount of a primary color with a secondary color. The two colors must be next to each other on the color wheel. Yellow orange is a tertiary color.

Which objects are tertiary colors?

There are different **shades** of each color. Shades are made by adding black to a color. This makes the color darker. **Tints** are made by adding white to a color. This makes the color look lighter. **Pastel colors** are lighter and look softer.

Which objects are pastel?

Everywhere we look, we see colors. Blue is the most common favorite color. What is your favorite color?

Can you find your favorite color in this photo?

Answer Key

Page 5　**Which objects reflect the color red?** The lobster, the roses, and the apple in the fruit basket all reflect the color red.

Page 7　**Which primary colors of light do you see in this rainbow?** Rainbows have all of the primary colors of light: red, green, and blue.

Page 9　**Which primary colors of pigment are in this painting?** There are two primary colors of pigment in this painting: red and yellow.

Page 11　**Which two colors shown here mix to make green?** Blue and yellow mix to make green.

Page 13　**Which of these objects match the color wheel?** The pinwheel and the lollipop match the color wheel.

Page 15　**Which of these team uniforms has complementary colors?** The cheerleading uniform has complementary colors.

Page 17　**Which objects are tertiary colors?** The bracelet and the pumpkin are both tertiary colors. The bracelet is blue green. The pumpkin is yellow orange.

Page 19　**Which objects are pastel?** The cupcakes and the eggs in the basket are pastel.

Glossary

absorbed (ab-ZORBD) Something that is absorbed is taken in by something else. Some colors are absorbed by objects.

complementary colors (kom-plih-MEN-tur-ee KUHL-urz) Complementary colors are colors that are opposite from each other on the color wheel. Yellow and purple are complementary colors.

pastel colors (pa-STEL KUHL-urz) Pastel colors are paler or lighter colors. You can add white to a color to make it pastel.

pigment (PIG-muhnt) A pigment is a substance that adds color to something. Paint is a kind of pigment.

primary colors (PRYE-mayr-ee KUHL-urz) Primary colors cannot be made by mixing other colors. The primary colors of light are red, green, and blue.

reflect (ri-FLEKT) To reflect is to bounce off an object. We see colors that reflect off objects.

secondary colors (SEK-uhn-dayr-ee KUHL-urz) Secondary colors are made by mixing primary colors. Orange, green, and violet are secondary colors.

shades (SHAYDZ) Shades are darker colors. Shades are made by adding black to a color.

tertiary colors (TUR-she-ayr-ee KUHL-urz) Tertiary colors are mixtures of primary colors and secondary colors that are next to each other on the color wheel. Yellow orange and blue green are tertiary colors.

tints (TINTZ) Tints are colors with white added to them. Pink and light blue are tints of red and blue.

To Learn More

Books

Blevins, Wiley. *Colors All Around.* South Egremont, MA: Red Chair Press, 2016.

Boothroyd, Jennifer. *Light Makes Colors.* Minneapolis, MN: Lerner Publications, 2015.

Rebman, Nick. *Who Is Wearing Blue? A Book about Colors.* Mankato, MN: The Child's World, 2017.

Web Sites

Visit our Web site for links about colors:
childsworld.com/links

Note to Parents, Teachers, and Librarians: We routinely verify our Web links to make sure they are safe and active sites. So encourage your readers to check them out!